Original title: Echoes of Twilight

Author: Kätriin Kaldaru
Editor: Jessica Elisabeth Luik
ISBN 978-9916-39-970-5

Echoes of Twilight

Kätriin Kaldaru

Evensong Reverie

In the hush of evening's grace,
Whispers soft in twilight's face,
Moonlight spills in silver streams,
Waking shadows from their dreams.

Stars ignite the velvet skies,
Silent echoes of goodbyes,
Night enshrouds in tender sweep,
Hours wade in peaceful sleep.

Breezes blend with whispers faint,
Nature's hymn, a lone monk's chant,
Heartbeats thrum in gentle tune,
Carried by a crescent moon.

Dimming Horizon

Sunset's glow begins to fade,
Blushing hues in twilight's shade,
Whispers of the oncoming night,
Softly douse the waning light.

Clouds streaked in colors bold,
Crimson tales of day retold,
As the west bids its farewell,
Stories in the twilight dwell.

Night descends with tender might,
Claiming day with velvety sight,
Stars align, a silent choir,
Singing songs of day's retire.

Day's Gentle Farewell

Lighter fades to deeper blue,
Evening paints each varying hue,
Shadows lengthen, gently sway,
Nighttime whispers come to play.

Silhouette of trees embrace,
Soft contours of day's grace,
Calm descends, a lullaby,
Cradling dusk with a sigh.

Birds retreat to nest and bough,
Twilight whispers soft and low,
Stars emerge, a scattered gem,
Lighting paths where dreams stem.

Twilight's Soft Embrace

Twilight wraps in silky fold,
Stories of the day retold,
Whispers travel on the breeze,
Through the rustling of the trees.

Moon ascends in regal flair,
Casting light both pale and fair,
Midnight flowers start to bloom,
Spreading scent in azure gloom.

Crickets start their serenade,
Notes of night in calm cascade,
Harmony of dark and light,
Eases through the birth of night.

Brushed with Twilight

The sky a canvas, hues entwined,
In twilight's arms, the colors bind.
Soft whispers of the night arise,
As day departs with tender sighs.

Stars awaken from their sleep,
In velvet skies their vigil keep.
Shadows stretch and gently weave,
Patterns dusk and dawn conceive.

Silent winds through treetops glide,
Mysteries in night they hide.
Moonlight scatters silver beams,
Draping earth in softened dreams.

Hushed Evening Murmurs

Evening's cloak of quiet grace,
Gentle murmurs fill the space.
Whispers in the cooling breeze,
Songs of night from swaying trees.

Crickets' chorus softly swells,
Echoing through dells and wells.
Lakes reflect the fading light,
Mirrors to the coming night.

Fireflies in silent flight,
Lanterns in the dusky light.
Nature's secrets softly speak,
In the night, the world is meek.

Softly Dimmed Skies

As daylight wanes and shadows grow,
In softly dimmed skies, a gentle glow.
The sun retreats with one last flare,
A whispered promise in the air.

Clouds of amber, streaks of gold,
Stories of the day unfold.
Soft and tender evening light,
Guides the weary world to night.

Birds on twilight breezes glide,
In the calm, they seek to hide.
The sky a warm embrace provides,
Softly dimmed, the night presides.

Dwindling Daylight

The sun's last kiss on hills so high,
As daylight dwindles, bids goodbye.
Colors merge in twilight's seam,
Awakening the night's own dream.

Silhouettes of distant trees,
Dance in twilight's gentle breeze.
Evening wraps the world in shade,
As light begins to softly fade.

Lanterned stars adorn the skies,
Guiding dreams, closing eyes.
In the glow of night's embrace,
Peaceful rest finds its place.

Radiance's Farewell

Sunset paints the skies in gold
Whispers of the evening told
Stars align in twilight's grace
Day's light fades without a trace

Crimson rays ignite the sea
Nature sighs in harmony
Shadowed hills bid light adieu
Nighttime skies in darkest hue

Breezes hum a final note
Over hills the echoes float
Glimmering with faintest gleam
Stars awake in twilight dream

Quiet Requiem of Eventide

Gentle hush that evening brings
Softest songs the twilight sings
Bidding farewell to the day
Nighttime casts its quiet sway

Muted tones of dusky skies
Whispers of the moonrise nigh
In the stillness, shadows creep
O'er the world, a tranquil deep

Stars composed in silent choir
Fading embers of the fire
Day's descent, a calm reprieve
As the night begins to weave

Wanes of the Horizon

Sunset’s glow on the horizon
Crimson hues in night's liaison
Golden hours drift away
Twilight spreads where shadows lay

Hues of purple blend with grey
Evening's quiet, calm display
As the sun dips from our sight
Stars emerge with gentle light

On the edge where day concedes
Nighttime's call, the heart heeds
Dusk envelops day's embrace
Wanes of horizon, night's trace

Susurrus of the Evenfall

Whispering winds through twilight's veil
Evening’s breath tells softest tale
Leaves in gentle rustle sing
Songs of dusk, they softly bring

Shades of dusk in hues obscure
Subtle tones that reassure
Quietude in day's decline
Nighttime's lull in dark design

Evenfall in tender sway
Bids the fleeting light away
Stars emerge, a shimmering thrall
In the susurrus of nightfall

Lucent Epiphanies

In the quiet dawn’s first gleam,
Whispers of a far-off dream,
Crystals dance in morning's flow,
Mystic truths the heart does know.

Radiant beams of sun’s embrace,
Light the soul, erase the trace,
Fragments of a world renewed,
Silent words in golden hue.

Waves of insight, soft and clear,
Visions bright, they draw so near,
Within the mind, a spark ignites,
To the soul, this light invites.

Event-time Stories

Underneath the twilight's grace,
Stories weave through time and space,
Moments hold a gentle power,
Echoed in the twilight hour.

Tales spun from the evening’s thread,
Voices of the past are spread,
Woven in the breeze's sigh,
Legend’s breath that will not die.

In the starlight, dreams unfold,
Mysteries that time has told,
Chronicles blend with the night,
Glowing softly, pure delight.

Whispers of Dusk

Softly twilight's shadows creep,
Whispers secrets, soft and deep,
Sunset’s glow in hues of red,
Murmurs of the day now shed.

Silent winds through leaves do rush,
Evening wrapped in gentle hush,
Stars begin their silent song,
Nighttime's whispers stretch so long.

Moon's embrace on silver streams,
Lulls the world in tender dreams,
Night whispers in quiet tones,
Echoes of the dusk-grown stones.

Fading Horizons

As the day begins to wane,
Horizons shrink, the shadows gain,
Colors blend in twilight’s paint,
Endless hues that seem so faint.

Memories in twilight's grasp,
With each brushstroke, moments clasp,
Fading light reveals the past,
Every glow will slowly last.

Distant skies in whispers sigh,
Boundaries merge, the night draws nigh,
Horizons fade in soft retreat,
Evening sighs in cool, sweet beat.

Shadows of the Setting Sun

In the quiet of the eve,
Golden hues begin to weave,
Through the trees and 'cross the sea,
Nature's art for all to see.

Night descends with velvet shroud,
Stars emerge, brilliant and proud,
Cool the air, the day is done,
Shadows of the setting sun.

Silent whispers fill the air,
Whispers soft and oh so fair,
Magical, the twilight's run,
Chasing shadows on the run.

Colors blend, a dreamy blur,
Twilight's stitch in night's great fur,
As the day’s last light has spun,
Shadows of the setting sun.

Whispers in the Dusk

Soft the sky in twilight's glow,
Hushed, the world begins to slow,
Whispers in the dusk do flow,
Secrets only night will know.

Shadows stretch and gently sway,
Dipping sun bids end to day,
In the hush, we find our way,
To where dreams and wishes lay.

Stars appear, a diamond dance,
Nature’s quiet, sweet romance,
In the dusk, a fleeting glance,
Memories in twilight's trance.

Soft and still, the world now seems,
Clothed in night's embrace of dreams,
Whispers in the dusk, so light,
Guide us through the fall of night.

The Fading Light

Amber hues, the sky ignites,
Day is turning into night,
Gently falls the fading light,
Into shadows, out of sight.

Mountains, rivers, trees align,
With the sun's last golden shine,
Peaceful is the grand design,
Nature's hand with brush divine.

Birds call softly, songs so sweet,
In the twilight, night they greet,
Fading light, a calm retreat,
Whispered winds, a soft heartbeat.

Twinkle stars in darkening skies,
In their glow, our spirit flies,
Daylight's end, a slow demise,
Promise in the night’s reprise.

Mystical Evening Murmurs

Breezes whisper through the leaves,
Soft the sound as daylight cleaves,
Evening murmurs, twilight breathes,
Nature's calm, our heart reprieves.

Crickets chirp in gentle rhyme,
Marking out the evening time,
Mystic moments, so sublime,
In night's woven, silent chime.

Moon ascends, a silvery mist,
Kisses earth with tender kiss,
Mystical, the world exists,
In the shadows night's dismissed.

Stars above in tranquil night,
Glowing softly, pure delight,
Evening murmurs, quiet light,
Guides us through till morning's bright.

Dimlit Dreams

In shadows deep where whispers flow,
Soft murmurs weave what night bestows,
A world where dimlit dreams take flight,
Beyond the reach of shadowed light.

Phantoms dance through twilight's grace,
In this ethereal, mystic space,
Lost in reveries' gentle seams,
We wander through our dimlit dreams.

Stars above in silence gleam,
Guiding us through night's serene theme,
In this realm where wishes stream,
We find solace in dimlit dreams.

Twilight's Summer Breeze

Beneath the sky in twilight's hold,
The summer breeze whispers bold,
Warmth and whispers intertwine,
A dance of seasons slow to unwind.

Golden hues in purple fade,
As day and dusk make their trade,
Leaves rustle with secrets told,
In twilight's embrace, a story unfolds.

Hand in hand, through fields we roam,
In this gentle twilight's tome,
Every breath a soft release,
In the summer twilight's breeze.

Fleeting Halo

A halo casts its fleeting glow,
Across the sky where soft winds blow,
Ephemeral beauty in twilight's clasp,
Moments tender, too soon passed.

Golden ring fades into night,
Echoes linger, brief in flight,
Transience marked by heaven's trace,
A brief encounter in twilight's grace.

In the quiet, whispers grow,
Tales of the halo's gentle show,
A fleeting glimpse of skies aglow,
In night, the memory's embers glow.

Hushed Glows

In the heart of night, where quiet grows,
Lies the secret of hushed glows,
Softly lit by Luna's tender grace,
Bathing earth in a celestial embrace.

Silent whispers in the dark,
Stars above begin to spark,
A canopy of dreams entwined,
In hushed glows, serenity we find.

Every shadow tells a tale,
In night's embrace, where dreams set sail,
A world alight with gentle flows,
We lose ourselves in hushed glows.

Softly Fallen Night

The moon whispers in dreamy tune,
Stars blink in an ancient rune,
The world in shadowed, soft repose,
Night's gentle breath bestows.

Owls call in melodies deep,
Winds through twilight secrets seep,
Crickets play their twilight song,
As hours stretch silent and long.

Footsteps fade on silver lane,
Whispers weave through window pane,
Candles flicker, shadows dance,
Lost in night's enchanting trance.

Mountains clothed in dark embrace,
Veil of night on nature's face,
A hush descends, serene and light,
Underneath the softly fallen night.

Subdued Gloaming

Sky in hues of quiet grey,
Waning light in soft display,
Day retreats with tender care,
Dusk's embrace is everywhere.

Leaves rustle with gentle sigh,
Birds take wing in violet sky,
Shadows stretch with calming grace,
Gloaming's hand on nature's face.

Rivers weave in twilight's fold,
Reflecting tales of whispers told,
A tranquil pulse in every beat,
Moments in subdued light meet.

Petals close and bow in prayer,
Evening's kiss in the cooling air,
Peace descends in subtle glow,
As subdued gloaming starts to grow.

Twilight’s Quietude

Echoes of the fading day,
In twilight's arms now gently sway,
Soft pastels in westward glow,
Silent serenade in tow.

Trees stand tall in shadowed line,
Night begins its slow incline,
Whispers in the cooling breeze,
Through the twilight, hearts find ease.

Lanterns flicker in the streets,
Dwelling in the dusk's retreats,
Calm enfolds the world anew,
In twilight's quietude, so true.

Moon ascends, a silver thread,
Dreams alight and softly spread,
Peaceful is the night's embrace,
In twilight's quietude, we trace.

Sunset's Lullaby

Sun dips low with golden sigh,
Drawing curtains on the sky,
Clouds like whispers gently part,
Heralding night with tender heart.

Birds sing soft their evening song,
As daylight hurries, not for long,
Horizon blushes one last hue,
In colors deep, the night is due.

Waves lap softly on the shore,
Echoes linger, ask for more,
Silence grows as stars appear,
Night's sweet song begins to clear.

Wind hums through the swaying trees,
A lullaby upon the breeze,
Day to night in softest glide,
Wrapped within sunset's gentle tide.

Purple Hues of Silence

In twilight's gentle hold, we find
The quiet whispers of the blind
A world embraced by evening's shroud
Where stars emerge from skies unbowed

The whispers of the violet breeze
Bring tales of distant, tranquil seas
Soft secrets shared in muted tone
In purple hues, we're not alone

Between the dusk and night's embrace
We chase the shadows, leave no trace
In stillness, dreams begin to bloom
Amid the fading light's perfume

Last Rays of the Horizon

The sun, a painter of the sky
With amber strokes as night draws nigh
Its brush caresses earth's edge line
As day folds into night, divine

Golden glimmers bid adieu
To fields of green, to skies of blue
The world in warm farewell soaks in
As twilight's curtain starts to thin

In these final moments, peace
A gentle pause before release
We stand in awe of fleeting light
As day dissolves into the night

Soft Spells of Sundown

When day begins to fold away
And shadows start their soft ballet
The sun whispers its last goodbyes
With hues of rose and lilac skies

Magic in the waning light
Spells of beauty, pure delight
A gentle sway of evening's breeze
Brushes leaves in dance with ease

Twilight woven threads unwind
Casting dreams into our mind
In the dusk, soft spells abound
As night descends without a sound

The Transition Hour

When light and dark begin to blend
And daytime's fervor finds its end
A pause within the fleeting hour
As twilight claims its gentle power

Shadows stretch and colors fade
A tranquil, quiet serenade
The sky, a canvas soft and rare
Painted with the evening air

The world in stillness contemplates
As night prepares to open gates
In this hour of sweet transition
We find repose, a soul’s rendition

Soft Lament of Evening

The night descends on whispered sighs,
A velvet cloak that blinds our eyes.
Stars like teardrops start to cling,
Soft lament, the dusk will sing.

Shadows weave their somber tales,
Through silent woods and moonlit trails.
Every breeze a breath, forlorn,
Grieving what the day has torn.

Lights from dwellings, faint and warm,
Battle back the night's cold charm.
Melancholy in the air,
Softly whispers everywhere.

Leaves are hushed in twilight's grip,
Nightingales their secrets sip.
In this hour, hearts find peace,
Evening's soft, lamented cease.

Crescent's Serenade

Upon the sky, a crescent light,
Guides the weary through the night.
Whispers from the stars above,
Serenade of distant love.

The silken thread of moonbeam's glow,
Ties a dream where shadows grow.
Waves of silver, gentle, sweet,
Underneath, the worlds do meet.

Trees embrace the lunar gleam,
Dancing softly in a dream.
Owls sing a midnight song,
Crescent light where hearts belong.

Silent rivers mirror skies,
Echoing the night’s disguise.
In the hush, a tender thread,
Crescent’s serenade is spread.

Muted Twilights

Muted twilights softly fall,
Casting shades on nature’s wall.
Quiet whispers fill the breeze,
Rustling through the sleepy trees.

Colors fade to twilight’s hue,
Bidding day a fond adieu.
Silver whispers touch the ground,
Hushed, where evening's peace is found.

Crickets hum their lullabies,
Stars awake with tender sighs.
Night doth feel so still, so deep,
In this glow, the world shall sleep.

Clouds embrace the dimming light,
As day gives way to gentle night.
Muted twilights, soft and true,
Paint the sky in shades anew.

Glimpses in Gloaming

In the gloaming, visions play,
Hints of dreams that hide away.
Twilight's fingers softly trace,
Glimpses of a secret grace.

Golden threads of sunset fade,
Into night, a soft cascade.
Whispers of the day now past,
Memories in shadows cast.

Winds that murmur through the leaves,
Tell of stories twilight weaves.
Ephemeral, this gentle dusk,
Gloaming's air, so sweetly hushed.

Stars begin their silent dance,
Lighting up the evening's trance.
In the gloaming, worlds unite,
Underneath the soft moonlight.

Fading Hues of Evening

The sky flares with a final blaze,
As sun dips low, the light does wane,
In twilight's grip, the color maze,
The day transforms to night again.

Shadows grow long, whispers soft,
The air is cool, the earth is still,
Above, the stars begin aloft,
The evening paints with quiet skill.

Horizon blushes, crimson fades,
A gentle veil of dusk unfurls,
The fleeting light, as life pervades,
In silent dance, the world it twirls.

The weary earth sighs deep and low,
Bathed in hues of dusk's embrace,
The twilight murmurs, soft and slow,
As darkness finds its sacred place.

Embers of the Day

As daylight wanes, its fire soft,
The amber glow begins to fade,
In sky, the hues are gently tossed,
The shadows lengthen, stars parade.

The world in quiet, winding down,
The echoes of the day subside,
In twilight's hold, the softest gown,
The evening whispers far and wide.

The embers burn with final glow,
The edges blur, the colors blend,
A lingering warmth, a tender show,
As night prepares its starlit mend.

The horizon's edge, a molten stream,
A molten sea of amber light,
The dusk enwraps in honeyed dream,
And ushers in the velvet night.

Whispering Nightfall

The night descends with quiet grace,
The stars ignite in velvet skies,
The moon, she rises, leaves her trace,
A silver gleam in sleepy eyes.

The whispers of the night unfold,
A symphony of calm and peace,
Within the dark, secrets are told,
As day's demands begin to cease.

The shadows stretch, the light recedes,
In harmony, the night proceeds,
Embracing dark, the world concedes,
To whisper's call and silent deeds.

Among the trees, the breezes sing,
The leaves rustle a soft refrain,
In night's embrace, the heart takes wing,
In darkness' cloak, the light remains.

Deepening Gloam

The air grows thick with deepening night,
As twilight fades to inky shroud,
The world resplendent in its flight,
Embraces stars from heaven bowed.

Silence whispers through the trees,
The gloam descends with hushed delight,
In soft embrace, the world agrees,
To welcome calm of endless night.

The fading hues of day, now gone,
As shadows stretch and merge in dark,
The night, it sings a soulful song,
A timeless, quiet, soothing arc.

The deepening gloam, it holds us tight,
In tender, soft, and lulling arms,
A canvas painted with the night,
Encloses us in gentle charms.

Evening Echoes

The breeze whispers low, through the twilight's embrace,
Colors merge softly, in a delicate chase,
Stars start to shimmer, in the vast open skies,
Mirroring dreams, in the twilight's soft sighs.

Shadows grow gently, as daylight retreats,
Footsteps grow lighter, on twilight-lit streets,
Nature's own chorus, hums a sweet tune,
As evening's echoes, dance under the moon.

In soft conversation, the crickets reply,
To dusk’s gentle calling, a lullaby,
Carried on whispers, the moments unfold,
Tales of the evening, quietly told.

Beneath the dim canopy, silence ensues,
Cloaking the landscape, in comforting hues,
Embers of daylight, slowly consume,
Giving their way, to the twilight's dark bloom.

With hearts gently swaying, to nightfall’s refrain,
Minds start to wander, on thoughts unchained,
Evening's embrace, holds us so near,
In the fading echoes, of daylight we hear.

Night's First Glimpse

As twilight surrenders, to evening’s embrace,
Shadows waltz softly, in intricate lace,
Stars start their vigil, across the dark sea,
Night's first glimpse, in harmony.

A gentle hush settles, on the world below,
Day's vibrant chorus, begins to slow,
Soft whispers of crickets, weave tales anew,
Under the night’s, deep-hued view.

Lanterns flicker, in windows around,
Casting warm glows, on the quiet ground,
Moonlight spills over, in silvery sprays,
Lighting the night, in mystical ways.

Beneath the starlight, the earth breathes slow,
Wrapped in the night’s, celestial glow,
Echoes of day, softly retreat,
As night’s first glimpse, layers complete.

Eyes to the heavens, in wonder we stare,
At the beauty that night, unfolds with care,
Infinite moments, in shadows and light,
Held within night’s, premier sight.

Shading to Night

Golden hues faded, as the sun dips low,
A canvas of twilight, begins to glow,
Clouds knit the sky, in a purple-gray flight,
Delicately shading, the world to night.

Whispers of wind, in the treetops high,
Carry sweet secrets, of day gone by,
Leisurely darkness, cloaks the land wide,
Drawing the curtain, of nightfall's tide.

Silhouettes dance, on horizon's edge,
Guided by stars, that silently pledge,
To guard all dreams, and watch from above,
Silent sentinels, of the night we love.

Fireflies glimmer, in fields pure and bright,
Tiny beacons, enlivening night,
Softly now fades, the last light of day,
As night takes its throne, in tranquil array.

Hearts beat gently, to night's gentle song,
Where dreams and reality, both belong,
In the soft shading, from day into night,
We find solace, in the moon’s gentle light.

Whispers in the Gloaming

The day begins its quiet end,
As shadows stretch and softly blend.
In the gloaming, whispers roam,
And beckon hearts to find their home.

Leaves rustle with a secret hymn,
While stars prepare to softly brim.
In twilight's grasp, the world transforms,
Embracing night with gentle norms.

Soft hues of purple, blue, and gold,
Weave stories that the dusk has told.
A tender hush descends so slow,
With whispers in the twilight's glow.

Quiet breezes kiss the land,
Drawing dreams with tender hands.
The gloaming hums its ancient song,
Inviting souls to drift along.

In the embrace of fading light,
The whispers soothe, dispel the night.
A tranquil promise softly sown,
In the gloaming, dreams are grown.

Twilight’s Gentle Caress

As day gives way to evening's shroud,
The colors fade, no longer proud.
Twilight's fingers softly trace,
A gentle touch upon the face.

The sky blushed with a tender pink,
Invites the world to pause and think.
In this embrace, the heart finds rest,
In twilight's gentle, soothing quest.

Shadows lengthen, drawing close,
Embracing trees in quiet prose.
The day's last breath, a soft caress,
Whispers dreams, the night to bless.

Stars awake in sky's deep blue,
A promise held in shimmering hue.
Twilight lingers, comforts all,
A tender moment before nightfall.

With twilight’s touch, the world at peace,
Night’s gentle cooing, sweet release.
The day departs with no distress,
In twilight's tender, gentle caress.

Fading Light Serenade

The sun dips low with a golden sigh,
Painting whispers on the sky.
Daylight bows to evening's charm,
A serenade, both soft and warm.

Birds begin their twilight songs,
Melodies the dusk prolongs.
Each note a promise of the night,
A serenade to fading light.

The air grows cool with night’s approach,
A soft retreat without reproach.
In the quiet, hearts find peace,
Fading light, a sweet release.

Stars begin their twinkling dance,
In twilight’s gentle, soft expanse.
The melody of night is played,
A lullaby that’s gently made.

In the hush of evening’s gaze,
The world sings in twilight’s praise.
A serenade that softly weaves,
In fading light, the soul believes.

Shadows of Dusk

As the sun sinks down the sky,
Shadows of dusk quietly lie.
Stretching long on field and tree,
A scene of tranquil mystery.

Twilight paints with gentle hues,
Soft pastels and deeper blues.
In the dusk, the world finds peace,
As day's demands steadily cease.

Silhouettes in twilight's gleam,
Stir the heart and mind to dream.
Shapes of night begin to form,
In shadows of dusk, they softly swarm.

Whispers of the night descend,
Promises of peace they send.
In the quiet, thoughts take flight,
On shadows dressed in fading light.

The day's last breath in twilight's care,
Surrenders softly to the air.
In shadows of dusk, we find our way,
To the tranquil end of another day.

Dimming Shadows

As daylight fades, the shadows grow,
Soft whispers in the twilight's flow.
With gentle grace, the night descends,
On moonlit paths, our journey wends.

Stars emerge like scattered seeds,
In the sky, where darkness feeds.
The world becomes a tranquil sea,
Where dreams and whispers wander free.

Candles flicker, casting light,
In this embrace of the night.
Old stories find their voice again,
In the dimming shadows, soft and ten.

Silent steps on ancient stone,
In the quiet, no one's alone.
Echoes of the past arise,
Beneath the vast and starry skies.

In the hush of evening's breath,
We find a peace in the day's death.
Time slows down, the minutes blend,
In dimming shadows, till night's end.

Nightfall Nuances

Colors fade as dusk arrives,
The day departs, but night revives.
Whispers in the evening air,
With nightfall's nuances everywhere.

Shadows dance on cobblestone,
The city draped in twilight's tone.
Stars peeking through the velvet black,
Guiding feet down pathways slack.

Lamps ignite with amber glow,
Glimmering on streets below.
Each corner hides a new delight,
In the nuances of the night.

The moon ascends in silver grace,
Illuminating each darkened space.
Nightbirds sing their evening song,
In the twilight, hearts belong.

Breathing in the cooler air,
Moments treasured, tender care.
The day's weight slips serene and slight,
In nightfall's tender nuanced light.

Glimpses of Nightfall

The horizon blends in hues of gray,
As fading light gives way to play.
Glimpses of nightfall start to show,
In softened steps of twilight's tow.

Streetlights cast their amber gleam,
In a world that's half a dream.
Each shadow holds a whispered tale,
In nightfall's grasp, our senses sail.

Leaves rustle with the evening breeze,
A symphony among the trees.
In the dimming, hearts find calm,
Nighttime's touch a soothing balm.

Windows glow with warm, soft light,
Beacons in the deepening night.
Silent streets and quiet lanes,
In nightfall's realm, peace remains.

Stars adorn the sky on high,
Tiny jewels in the vast, deep sky.
Glimpses of an endless sea,
Nightfall's gift to you and me.

Emerging Night

As the sun dips low, shadows spawn,
Dusk's embrace, a quiet dawn.
Colors fade to shades of night,
Emerging softly, pale moonlight.

Twilight whispers secrets old,
Stories in the stars foretold.
Night emerges from the day,
In gentle, silent, dark array.

Lanterns flicker, streets unwind,
Paths of wonder, undefined.
In the day's retiring gleam,
Night awakens like a dream.

Echoes softly fill the air,
Peaceful moments, everywhere.
In the quiet, hearts align,
With the emerging night's design.

Darkness brings a tender hush,
In the starlit, velvet brush.
Time slows in this soft display,
As night emerges, shadows sway.

Evanescent Light

With a glow, the day retreats,
Fading softly, dimming night,
Shadows stretch and twilight greets,
Stars awaken with their light.

In the cloak of twilight's shroud,
Memories wane, gently sway,
Silent whispers, softly loud,
In the dim, the heart's ballet.

Winds caress the evening's veil,
Leaves in breezes dance and twirl,
Mysteries in moonlight trail,
Night commands its starry whirl.

Transient beauty, fleeting beam,
Moments lost to dark's embrace,
Nature's soft, enchanting dream,
Ephemeral, a tender grace.

In the calm of night's descent,
Worlds unseen in shadows hide,
Evanescent light, content,
Guides the souls where dreams reside.

Twilight's Prelude

The sun dips low with gentle grace,
A golden hug, the earth's embrace.
Shadows grow as light takes leave,
A painted sky at twilight's eve.

Whispers of the day now done,
Mingle with the night begun.
Stars bind the sky in threads so fine,
A twilight prelude, so divine.

Gloaming's Grace

In the fleeting moments, softly bright,
Gloaming casts a tender light.
Colors wane in hues of grey,
Softly marking end of day.

Leaves rustle in a gentle hush,
As day gives way to evening's blush.
Nature hums a quiet tune,
Underneath the rising moon.

Murmurs of Dusk

The quiet whisper of the dusk,
Air scented with the earth's musk.
Birds sing their final song,
As night plods gladly along.

The sky, a canvas darkening,
Moon and stars are harkening.
Silence grows in shadows' wake,
As dreams begin to softly take.

Night's Soft Arrival

The day, now gone, leaves a trace,
Of twilight's gentle, fading face.
Stars glitter in the velvet sky,
As evening sings its lullaby.

Soft whispers of the night's embrace,
Wrap the world in darkened grace.
Peaceful moments, silent, still,
Under moon's ethereal thrill.

Twilight’s Embrace

Sun dips low with gentle grace
Purple hues take daylight’s place
Stars ignite in velvet skies
Softly, night’s cool whispers rise

Moon ascends with silver gown
Casting dreams on sleepy town
Quiet peace in twilight’s hold
Stories yet to be foretold

Evening’s Palette

Brushstrokes paint the evening sky
Crimson, gold - a lover’s sigh
Clouds weave patterns, wild and free
Nature's art for all to see

Dusk unveils her secret hues
Blending pinks with twilight blues
Shadows dance ‘neath fading light
Canvas rich in falling night

Subdued Skies

Grey above in twilight's shroud
Soft and still, no voice too loud
Whispers borne on evening breeze
Calm as song of swaying trees

Violet melt in horizon's fold
Starlets pierce through dusk of old
Boundless peace in muted shades
Day descends where silence wades

Twilight’s Murmurings

Gloaming whispers, day’s farewell
Echoes where the shadows dwell
Crickets chirp in night’s debut
Symphony 'neath twilight's hue

Whispering leaves, a tranquil tune
Crescent smiles a slender moon
Magic found in dimming light
Twilight’s murmurings of night

Dusk's Enigma

Shadows stretch and softly blend,
As day concedes its light.
Whispers of the evening send,
Secrets to the night.

Crimson hues in twilight sky,
Kiss the world goodnight.
In the hush, the whispers fly,
Held by fading light.

Mysteries in darkness bloom,
As stars begin to sway.
In the cool and gentle gloom,
Night takes hold of day.

Serenade of Sundown

Golden beams of sunlight fade,
Curtains drawn by night.
Nature’s song, a serenade,
Softly dims the light.

Birds sing out their final verse,
Trees sway in delight.
Evening’s calm, a gentle curse,
Under twilight’s might.

Moon ascends in silent grace,
Stars join in the tune.
In this quiet, sacred space,
Lay the dreams of June.

Starlit Twilight

Evening cloaks in velvet blue,
Stars like secrets shine.
Night unfurls, a world anew,
With whispers so divine.

Silver beams on silken thread,
Weave a tranquil sight.
Glimmers where the day has bled,
Into starlit night.

Cosmic dances, twinkling bright,
Guide us through the dark.
In the stillness of twilight,
Dreams ignite their spark.

Whispers at Sundown

Sun descends in hues of gold,
Night begins its dance.
Stories in the dusk retold,
In twilight's soft trance.

Crickets chime a melody,
Breeze begins to sigh.
Whispers hum in symphony,
Beneath the starlit sky.

Dusk enfolds the day's embrace,
Nighttime's gentle gait.
In the quiet, whispers trace,
Paths to dreams of fate.

Secrets in the Half-Light

Twilight whispers secrets old,
Veils of dusk, with stories told,
Glowing skies in hues of gold,
Ancient mysteries unfold.

Silhouettes in shadow play,
Figures blend into the haze,
Half-light shows the night's array,
Secrets hide in dusky glaze.

Soft and silent, secrets weave,
Through the gloam and past the eve,
Truths that only dusk can leave,
In the stillness, hearts believe.

Clouds adorn the purple sky,
Nighttime birds begin to fly,
In the half-light, spirits sigh,
Dreams unseen to waking eye.

As the day to night gives way,
Echoes of the twilight stay,
Secrets in the half-light pray,
For the dawn of a new day.

Whispers of the Waning Sun

As the sun begins its fall,
Golden hues upon the wall,
Daylight whispers, soft and small,
Nighttime spreads its quiet thrall.

Gentle murmurs fill the air,
Shadows lengthen everywhere,
Crickets start their evening prayer,
Moonrise paints the sky with care.

Waning light on rivers gleam,
Nature sighs in twilight's dream,
Stars awaken, small and keen,
In the dusk, they softly beam.

Whispers float on twilight breeze,
Through the rustling of the trees,
Day's farewell with tender ease,
Hints of night in every crease.

Time for sleep and dreams begun,
Memories of day now spun,
In the whispers of the sun,
Life's eternal, quiet run.

Murmurs of Misty Dusk

Misty dusk, a veil so thin,
Softly cloaks the world within,
Evening sighs where light has been,
Nighttime songs just now begin.

Shadows blend in hues of grey,
Murmurs of the fading day,
Whispers in the twilight stay,
Guiding night in gentle sway.

Stars reveal their silver flame,
Moonlight dons a quiet name,
In the dusk, no two the same,
Murmurs play a shadow game.

Coolness of the evening's breath,
Signals day’s impending death,
In the hush, a soft bequeath,
Misty dusk, in peace and wreath.

Moments wrapped in twilight's care,
Magic lingers in the air,
Murmurs of the dusk declare,
Nighttime's secrets, pure and fair.

Shadows of Evening

The dusk spreads its wings, so vast and high,
As twilight paints the fading sky.
Whispers of night through trees do weave,
In shadows of evening, dreams believe.

Winds murmur softly, a lullaby sweet,
Where shadows and sunlight gently meet.
Stars slowly wake in their silent parade,
As day to night begins to fade.

The horizon blushes, a final gleam,
With hues of gold, in a waking dream.
Twilight whispers secrets in the breeze,
Shadows of evening, memories seize.

Night's curtain draws, the world a stage,
In soft repose, a calm engage.
In shadows of evening, worlds unfold,
In whispers of starlight, tales are told.

Tranquil Night's Edge

At the edge of night, where silence sings,
Moonlight dances on silver wings.
The world in hushed whispers softly sways,
In the tranquil night, dreams softly lay.

Stars adorn the velvet sky so grand,
Silent guardians of ancient lands.
In the stillness, hearts find their rest,
On tranquil night's edge, whispered caress.

Soft tendrils of mist weave through the air,
In the twilight, a moment so rare.
Bathed in the glow of the lunar guide,
Tranquil embraces, hearts open wide.

The night cradles the weary and worn,
Promises of a gentle morn.
In tranquil night's edge, peace is found,
In every echo, a gentle sound.

Twilight's Farewell

Twilight whispers its goodbyes,
With hues of fire in fading skies.
The day retreats in amber shades,
As twilight's farewell gently fades.

Cicadas hum their evening song,
In twilight's arms, where dreams belong.
The horizon sighs, a final glow,
In twilight's farewell, hearts beat slow.

The stars emerge in the quiet dark,
Each one a tender, glowing spark.
With every breath, the moment still,
Twilight's farewell, a gentle thrill.

In the quiet, shadows softly play,
Marking the end of another day.
Twilight's farewell, a silent prayer,
For peace and love everywhere.

Day’s Last Kiss

The sun descends with a gentle grace,
Bestowing a kiss on nature’s face.
Golden hues on leaves do glisten,
Day's last kiss, hearts do listen.

In the hush of the evening glow,
Whispers of day, soft and slow.
Embrace of twilight, tender and sweet,
Day’s last kiss, where dreams meet.

Skies aflame with colors bold,
A story of day in shades untold.
Day’s last kiss, serene and warm,
A promise kept through the calm.

As night descends, stars awake,
In the silence, dreams softly take.
In day’s last kiss, find solace deep,
In the embrace of night, hearts sleep.

Dusky Symphonies

In the twilight's tender grasp,
Whispers dance across the night.
Melodies of shadows' clasp,
Craft a symphony's delight.

Starry notes in twilight's veil,
Play a tune of gentle dreams.
As the winds begin their trail,
Soul and sky are stitched in seams.

Crickets' song and owls' call,
Harmonize with evening's breath.
In this choir, I feel it all,
Life and dusk converse with death.

Candles flicker through the dark,
Voices blend in quiet grace.
Night's serenade leaves its mark,
On the heart in soft embrace.

Moonlight writes its silver song,
On the canvas of the skies.
Where the midnight dreams belong,
Underneath the heavens' eyes.

Fading Daylight

A blush of gold and scarlet hues,
As daylight sighs its final notes.
The sunset bids a soft adieu,
While twilight drapes its velvet coats.

Shadows stretch and merge afar,
Chasing light to where it fades.
Evening beckons every star,
Till the first of night invades.

Birdsong whispers short goodbyes,
To the sun's retreating glow.
As the dusky twilight spies,
Night begins its gentle flow.

Silver whispers through the leaves,
Dancing in the waning light.
Softly twilight weaves and weaves,
Tapestries of coming night.

Purpling skies in silent mime,
Hold the whispers of the dusk.
As the fading day's new chime,
Bathes the night in fragrant musk.

Silent Crepuscule

Velvet skies in twilight's shade,
Hold the day in tender arms.
Where the silent whispers fade,
Resting now from daylight's charms.

Evening breathes her gentle touch,
O'er the landscape, calm and clear.
Nighttime gathers stars in clutch,
In the silence, drawing near.

Gloaming hour's stealthy stride,
Wraps the world in soft caress.
Making dark and light collide,
In a symbiotic dress.

Luna's glow in silver threads,
Weaves the night in mystic light.
As the world in quiet treads,
Into realms of tranquil night.

Crepuscule's serene embrace,
Lulls the weary day to rest.
Leaving in the stars a trace,
Of its silent, gentle quest.

Gleam of Evening

Evening drapes in hues of gold,
Softly whispers to the dusk.
Stories of the day retold,
In the air a fragrant musk.

Lanterns light the twilight's path,
Guiding shadows through the night.
In the gleam, no sign of wrath,
Only peace in soft moonlight.

Crickets sing their serenade,
Echoes through the cooling breeze.
Evening's gleam begins to fade,
As the darkness starts to tease.

Stars like diamonds start to glow,
Scattered on the velvet sky.
In their light, the secrets flow,
Of the night and day's goodbye.

Dusky hues and twilight gleam,
Paint the earth in shades of grace.
In this quiet, endless dream,
Evening smiles, a calm embrace.

Softened Sunlight

Glimmering gently through the trees,
Whispering through the golden leaves,
A softened cry of nature's breeze,
Embracing all that it perceives.

Sunlight dances on the streams,
Colliding with our tender dreams,
In hues that paint the sky aglow,
In melodic, peaceful themes.

Whispers of the morning rise,
Adorning dawn in soft surprise,
With every touch, the warmth it brings,
Mirroring the azure skies.

In tender waves of light it flows,
Over every petal grows,
A gentle reminder of earth’s song,
Where love's true essence softly glows.

Through the veil of morning mist,
Luminous hues that softly kissed,
The softened sunlight calms us all,
In every dewdrop's tender bliss.

Dusky Wonders

As twilight casts its hazy charm,
Softly wraps the world in calm,
Silhouettes in dusky framings,
Nature holding out its arm.

Shadows lengthen as light fades,
In this mystic dusky glade,
Silent whispers of the night,
In twilight's gentle serenade.

Stars peeking through velvet skies,
Glimmering with ancient ties,
Dusky wonders paint the eve,
With celestial lullabies.

Evening's breath in cool reprise,
Underneath the darkening skies,
Every corner, softly draped,
In dusky wonders, hearts arise.

For in the hush, the world at rest,
With gentle awe, our souls are blessed,
Dusky wonders, dreams take flight,
In nature's tranquil, warm caress.

Night’s Onset

As daylight bids a soft farewell,
The evening casts its mystic spell,
Night’s onset gently creeps to shore,
With secrets only stars could tell.

The horizon blushes in its wake,
As darkness blooms for dreams to take,
Midnight whispers fill the air,
In night’s embrace, our hearts partake.

Slowly spreads the evening air,
A cloak of stars that lights the wear,
Silence hums a lullaby,
Night’s onset holds us unaware.

The moon ascends in silent grace,
A gentle smile upon her face,
Night's mystery unfolds the path,
In shadows dark, we find our place.

Crickets sing their ancient songs,
As twilight leads the night along,
In the onset of the night,
We feel the world where we belong.

Twinkle of Twilight

In the stillness of the eve,
Twilight spreads its silken weave,
Cloaking earth in quiet dreams,
A moment's breath as day takes leave.

Stars emerge in soft delight,
Little beacons in the night,
Twinkle of twilight gently shines,
Guiding hearts with subtle light.

Whispers of the winds' embrace,
Lift our spirits, slow in pace,
Twinkles in the twilight gleam,
In every corner, time and space.

Ebbing tides and rustling trees,
Carry tales upon the breeze,
Twinkle of twilight, timeless, free,
Echoes of eternity.

In these tender twilight hours,
Bound by moon and starlit flowers,
Twinkle of twilight's tender kiss,
Lulling us to tranquil bliss.

Evening's Reverie

The sky in hues of crimson, fades to dark,
Whispers of the wind, gentle as a lark,
Stars emerge, like diamonds strewn afar,
In evening's reverie, beneath the stellar arc.

Twilight dances, in shadows of the trees,
Soft and warm, the night begins to ease,
Moonlight glimmers, as silent as the seas,
A tranquil night, riding evening's breeze.

The day, now past, in slumber lies,
Dreams take wing, in night's embrace it flies,
Quiet moments, like embers in the skies,
Evening's reverie, in a world so wise.

Luna's glow, a guide through azure days,
Gentle whispers, in evening's peaceful ways,
Nature's song, in soft and silent praise,
Wonders unfold, in night's gentle rays.

Rest now, hearts, in calm and tender night,
In evening's reverie, find your light,
Dreams and stars, forever intertwined tight,
A serene dance, till dawn's early light.

Beyond the Sundown

Orange lingers, as the sun dips low,
Shadows stretch, with a gentle flow,
Beneath the heavens, where soft winds blow,
Mysteries awaken, beyond the sundown's glow.

Silhouette of mountains, bathed in twilight's kiss,
A serene moment, not a thing to miss,
Whispered secrets, in the evening's bliss,
Dreams arise, in a night like this.

Galaxies flourish, beyond the eye's reach,
Silent wisdom, they silently teach,
In the hush of night, lessons we beseech,
Beyond the sundown, the stars impeach.

Nature's hush, a silken symphony,
In this quiet realm, hearts are free,
Beneath the twilight, spirit's decree,
Boundless, endless, as the open sea.

Journey onward, through the twilight's gate,
Past the horizon, toward our fate,
In the dusk, dreams resonate,
Beyond the sundown, where stardust waits.

Nightfall Murmurs

As light dissolves, and shadows play,
Nightfall murmurs, in a soft array,
Tender whispers, in twilight's sway,
A gentle calm, as day slips away.

Breeze caresses, with a loving wisp,
Leaves rustle, in a nocturnal crisp,
Whispers echo, in an endless lisp,
Nightfall murmurs, in a peaceful dip.

Stars appear, in a velvet sky,
Silent watchers, as dreams drift by,
Moonbeams dance, with a shy sigh,
Nightfall murmurs, with a lullaby.

Owls hoot softly, in the velvet dome,
In the night’s embrace, we’re not alone,
Dreams and shadows, together roam,
Nightfall murmurs, calling us home.

Rest in stillness, till the break of morn,
In nightfall's arms, be gently borne,
Murmurs soothe, from dusk till dawn,
In dream’s embrace, till a new day’s yawn.

Dimlit Dreams

Amber hues, as daylight fades,
In dimlit dreams, in twilight's shades,
Silent paths, in moonlit glades,
A journey starts, as memory parades.

Whispers float, in a star-kissed night,
Soft as feathers, in silver light,
Dreams take flight, so pure, so bright,
In dimlit dreams, hearts ignite.

Shadows paint, in gentle streams,
A canvas pure, of hopes and schemes,
In the quiet, where everything seems,
We find ourselves, in dimlit dreams.

Mystic realms, where stardust gleams,
In the quiet dusk, emotion teems,
Boundless night, where everything redeems,
A tender voyage, in dimlit dreams.

Restful night, in soft embrace,
Dimlit dreams, a sacred place,
In silence, find a gentle grace,
Till dawn arrives, with a tender trace.

Twilight's Whisper

The sky unfolds in hues of blue,
The day and night begin to fuse.
In twilight's whisper, soft and clear,
A gentle call for stars to cheer.

The world in shadows, calm and still,
A respite from the daily drill.
Whispers through the leaves and trees,
Carrying tales on evening's breeze.

Mountains dark against the sky,
Birds return as light says goodbye.
In this moment, time suspends,
With twilight’s touch, the earth attends.

Silent waters mirror glow,
From dusk to dawn, their secrets flow.
As twilight whispers soft and rare,
Lost in dreams, beyond compare.

Evening blooms with silent grace,
Stars emerge to take their place.
Twilight's whisper, light as air,
A lullaby beyond compare.

Silent Evening Reflections

Daylight fades, the shadows creep,
Silent secrets, evening keeps.
Mirror lakes of twilight's realm,
Calming whispers at the helm.

Stars awake from hidden veil,
Arms of night on earth prevail.
In the quiet, thoughts arise,
Painting pictures in the skies.

Reflections in the twilight's core,
Silent echoes of folklore.
Evening, still and softly bright,
Guides us through the gentle night.

Whispers lost on breezes mild,
Tales of dreams and days compiled.
In the silence, hearts find peace,
Under moonlight's soft release.

Silent evening's tranquil charms,
Wraps the earth in gentle arms.
Reflections linger, night resumes,
Cradling dreams in starry blooms.

Glimmering Gloam

Twilight spreads its golden veil,
Soft and warm, the evening's tale.
Glimmering in gentle waves,
In the gloam, the heart behaves.

Shadows weave through fields of light,
As day succumbs to restful night.
Stars begin their dance on high,
Greeting night with a dreamy sigh.

Every leaf and blade of grass,
Catches whispers as they pass.
In the gloaming, peace is found,
Every sound a soothing bound.

Silent rivers, muted calls,
Evening's light as darkness falls.
Glimmering with tranquil care,
Whispered secrets fill the air.

Gloaming glows with twilight's kiss,
A momentary ethereal bliss.
In the stillness, hearts adorning,
Glimmers herald night's first morning.

Veil of the Setting Sun

As the sun dips low and fades,
Casting long and gentle shades.
Veil of hues from gold to dun,
Wraps the earth, the setting sun.

Birds' last songs before the night,
Meld with twilight's tender light.
Veil descends in whispers sweet,
Nighttime calls from day's retreat.

Mountains silhouette the sky,
Veiled in dusk, the eve draws nigh.
The world's awash in twilight's band,
As shadows take the upper hand.

Stars emerge through veil so soft,
Guiding us where dreams aloft.
Setting sun's farewell embrace,
Signals night’s serene replace.

Veil of evening, calm and blue,
Promises of dreams anew.
With the setting sun's descent,
Night begins its sweet present.

Milton Keynes UK
Ingram Content Group UK Ltd.
UKHW022139310524
443357UK00004B/95

9 789916 399705